21 Days to a More Secure Happy You

Based on two psychologically sound subconscious reprogramming exercises.

By Molly

"You don't attract what you want – you attract what you are." – Unknown

Welcome to a 21-day journey designed to pull the rug out from under your subconscious mind's worst tricks and replace its chaos with a solid foundation of confidence, peace, and self-worth. Sounds good, right? But let's be clear—this workbook isn't about surface-level positivity or half-hearted affirmations. We're diving deep, rewiring the very beliefs that keep you stuck, unsure, or quietly self-sabotaging.

Negative self beliefs can ruin relationships in several ways. First, you can be the one behaving badly. Secondly, your negative self beliefs could lead you to getting into relationships with the wrong people.

Over the next three weeks, you'll be introduced to two simple yet profoundly effective exercises. These aren't random self-help fluff; they're tools to uncover the sneaky, limiting beliefs your subconscious has been clutching like a bad playlist on repeat. And better yet, they'll help you replace those outdated hits with empowering, feel-good mental tracks.

So, Why Mess with the Subconscious?

Because it's running the show, that's why. Your subconscious mind is a 24/7 machine, quietly shaping your thoughts, feelings, and actions based on all the experiences and beliefs you've absorbed over the years. Some are helpful. Most, let's be honest, are not. Most of them were formed before you were eight – so some might not even be valid anymore.

Think about those whispers in the back of your mind: "I'm not good enough," or "I'm ugly," or the ever-classic "I'm stupid." Where do they come from? That's your subconscious, and over time, those whispers morph into a full-blown megaphone, dictating how you see yourself, your relationships, and your potential.

The good news? Beliefs can be rewritten. Your subconscious isn't set in stone—it's more like a chalkboard covered in old scribbles. With the right tools (like this book), you can wipe it clean and start fresh.

Why 21 Days? Because Habits Take Time

Science and psychology agree that creating real, lasting change takes repetition. That's why this program spans three weeks. It's the sweet spot for introducing new patterns of thinking while disrupting the old ones. Think of it like installing an update on your brain's operating system—slow, steady, and well worth the effort.

This isn't a magic wand. It's not about throwing glittery affirmations at your problems. This work goes deeper. We're targeting the roots of those pesky negative beliefs so you can uproot them for good.

What You'll Get Out of This

By the end of this journey, you'll start noticing shifts—not fireworks, but quiet, undeniable changes. Maybe it's the absence of that nagging self-doubt or a newfound sense of ease when making decisions. Maybe it's feeling less anxious, more secure, and more you. Maybe you'll start feeling like you can work through problems instead of running away. Or perhaps you'll feel more confident thinking "this isn't for me" instead of working harder to prove your worth.

As these new beliefs settle in, they'll start shaping your reality in subtle yet profound ways. Confidence feels natural. Happiness doesn't seem so elusive. And that voice in your head finally starts being kind.

How This Works

This isn't a marathon. Each daily exercise takes 20–25 minutes tops. All you need is consistency. Do the work, show up daily, and let the exercises do their thing. If you miss a day, no guilt—just pick up where you left off. But I must reiterate that it's most effectively when do it every day with no misses.

And yes, you'll probably face some resistance. Old beliefs don't go quietly. But every time you push through, you're reinforcing a new narrative: one where you're capable, worthy, and in charge of your own story.

Before you dive in, here's something to sit with: if you don't confront the subconscious, it'll keep sabotaging your happiness on autopilot. Isn't it time to take the wheel?

Is This Workbook for You?

Read through the following collection of scenarios. If any of them resonate with you, this book is for you!

You feel stuck in a cycle of self-doubt and negative thinking

Do you constantly question your worth or abilities? Perhaps you feel like no matter how much you achieve, it's never enough to shake off that inner critic. This book will guide you in breaking free from limiting beliefs that keep you from reaching your full potential.

You're anxious or insecure in relationships

Do you find yourself worrying about rejection, even in stable relationships? If you struggle with insecurity, jealousy, or fear of abandonment, the exercises in this book will help you identify and release the deep-seated beliefs that drive these feelings, helping you feel more secure and at peace.

You battle with imposter syndrome or fear of failure

Does the thought of failure keep you from taking risks or pursuing your goals? Imposter syndrome can make you feel like an outsider in your own life. This book offers techniques to replace feelings of inadequacy with genuine confidence.

You're weighed down by past traumas or wounds

Do you carry pain from past experiences that you can't seem to let go? If you find it difficult to move past old hurts or believe you're "broken" because of them, this book will help you reframe those experiences and start to heal.

You're tired of being controlled by anxiety

Do daily worries leave you feeling mentally exhausted? This book provides tools to reprogram the thoughts and beliefs that keep anxiety alive, helping you feel calm, grounded, and more capable of facing life's challenges.

You want to boost your self-worth and self-acceptance

Do you struggle to love and accept yourself? If you're often overly critical or harsh on yourself, the 21-day journey in this book will help you cultivate self-acceptance and appreciation, allowing you to feel worthy of happiness and success.

Are you going through a breakup and struggling to get over it, fearing it was all your fault or you're not worthy?

Breakups can activate core negative wounds and have us feeling all kinds of negative things about ourselves. This workbook will help you get over the insecurities the breakup has woken in you.

You've tried affirmations and positive thinking, but they don't stick

If you've ever tried affirmations or self-help that's because affirmations don't work on the subconscious alone. This book provides a more in-depth approach. It addresses the root causes of negativity and self-doubt, helping you make lasting changes rather than temporary improvements.

You feel awkward and uncomfortable in social situations, thinking people don't like you or you don't fit in

Social awkwardness can stem from negative self-beliefs which this workbook will help to reverse.

You want to break free from self-sabotaging patterns

Do you often find yourself repeating the same unhelpful behaviors? Whether it's procrastination, negative self-talk, or unhealthy relationships, this book offers strategies to help you rewire your mind and make choices that support your well-being.

"You don't attract what you want – you attract what you are." - Unknown

This book was designed to be a concise info-sharing piece paired with two daily subconscious reprogramming exercises to be completed over 21 days. You can use the available space in the workbook to record your responses, or you can use an external journal.

Before you start the exercises to reprogram your subconscious, it's important to understand the reason behind the exercises.

I'll try to break it down in simple terms.

The subconscious mind is like a huge storage system. It quietly holds all our beliefs, emotions, memories, and past experiences—even the ones we may not consciously remember. It works behind the scenes to guide our behaviors, habits, and emotional reactions without us having to think about it directly.

You know that one time someone said or did something, and you felt the emotions rising and had a major reaction? There's nothing wrong with you. The situation triggered something your subconscious has been holding onto and bam, it fought back with a reaction.

The thing about the subconscious is that by the time we turn 8, it's decided everything it thinks about relationships, other people, the world, and our feelings/behaviors and actions in general.

This is how we develop our attachment style. Now, an 8-year-old has the reigns and controls how you think, feel, and act in all situations in life. The subconscious isn't wrong per se. It's just developed strategies to keep you safe. But the reality is that some of those strategies don't keep you safe – in fact, they turn your worst fears and insecurities into self-fulfilling prophecies.

An example scenario to illustrate.

You're starting a new job or your first day at school and you're riddled with anxiety. You don't consider yourself a people person because you assume people don't like you and you don't fit in.

As a result, you already expect people not to want to talk to you or to be funny towards you before you've even arrived on your first day of work/school. This is anxiety at play.

With all this in your mind, you arrive at your first day and you're withdrawn, quiet, and awkward. This is because you don't want people to notice you because *eh, they're not going to like you anyway* or *won't want to talk to you* or you're *just not going to fit in.*

The other people in the room see you physically distancing yourself, not talking, and acting awkward, so they keep their distance thus reinforcing the idea in your mind that they don't like you and don't want to talk to you. But in fact, they're just reading you and likely keeping their distance because of that.

And this is how a story your subconscious has told you about yourself becomes a reality. The trick is to change the stories your subconscious is telling you so that your behaviors and "energy" or "vibe" change - so all other areas of your life change too.

This is just one example that can extend to all types of negative thoughts and feelings.

For instance, you may think: *I didn't have the perfect marriage/relationship because I'm not good enough or I'm defective.*

This is based on the subconscious telling you these things and it's impossible to find happiness if you're wallowing in a pit of negative thought loops. If you believe you're not good enough, you'll behave that way and others will start reading that believe it too. It's a nasty, nasty cycle.

The interesting and most awful thing about the subconscious mind is that it controls 97% of all our thoughts and emotions. And it's a creature of habit.

Even if the negative thought loops are uncomfortable and depressing, the subconscious over the years has become used to that and considers it a comfort zone (the devil you know kind of thing) so even if you want to inspire positive change, the subconscious will fight hard to hang onto its comfort zone. It will ramp up its efforts to bring up those core wounds to keep you from changing - not because it's making a good decision for you but because it is scared.

It doesn't understand the alternative. You must teach it the alternative and that's called subconscious reprogramming. It takes 21 days to change the subconscious. I'd recommend 42.

Examples of core wounds:

I am not good enough
I am different
I don't belong
I am not liked
I am abandoned
I am not loveable
I am not appreciated
I am not interesting
I am unwanted
I am unworthy
I am not noticed
I am unheard/unseen
I am trapped

I am stupid
I am ugly
I am disconnected
I am too much

This is just the tip of the iceberg – there are many and you'll likely know what yours are, but don't worry, I'll share a simple exercise with you to get to the bottom of yours if you're unsure.

When we go through difficult or stressful experiences, especially if they're ongoing, the subconscious mind can start building negative thoughts and belief patterns based on those experiences.

Here's how it works:

Stress and Fear Responses

If we go through a lot of stressful situations, our subconscious mind starts to expect stress. It holds onto feelings of anxiety or fear, even when things are fine because it's trying to protect us by staying "on guard."

Repetitive Negative Thoughts and Feelings of Lack

When we experience negative emotions (like self-doubt or worry) repeatedly, the subconscious mind treats those thoughts as normal. Over time, it becomes easier for the mind to focus on the negative rather than the positive, making it feel natural to be worried, tired, or even hopeless.

Emotional Suppression

Often, if we avoid or ignore difficult emotions, they don't actually go away—they get stored in the subconscious. Over time, this buildup can create feelings of emotional exhaustion, burnout, or even depression, as the mind tries to "hold" everything in. This sometimes also happens if a person uses activities or projects, chores, and tasks to distract from negative feelings.

Why Subconscious Reprogramming is Important

Medication can help us feel better by managing symptoms, but it often doesn't address the root beliefs and emotional patterns that contribute to how we feel. I am not saying you shouldn't take medications if you've been prescribed them. I am recommending that you add emotional work to the process of getting to a place of feeling good about yourself and your life.

This is where subconscious reprogramming comes in. Reprogramming means working directly with the subconscious to release and replace negative thought patterns with healthier, more positive ones. And when you're thinking in a healthier more positive way, things start to take a turn in your life – you're also more likely to attract healthy and positive people and scenarios into your life.

By using subconscious reprogramming techniques, we can:

Replace Negative Beliefs

Changing beliefs like "I'm not good enough" to "I am capable and deserving" at a subconscious level helps shift how we feel about ourselves in a way that we notice, others notice, and the world around us starts to respond to.

Reduce Automatic Negative Thoughts

When we work with the subconscious, we can learn to stop immediately expecting stress or worry, making it easier to handle challenges calmly and without them unbalancing our entire lives.

Relieve Stored Emotions

Exercises that help us process and release past emotions allow the subconscious mind to "let go" of old hurts, reducing emotional exhaustion and burnout.

General Sense of Happiness and Well-being

When you relieve that 8-year-old in your subconscious of the mammoth responsibility of having to keep you safe by pre-empting every negative thing, you'll feel a sense of general happiness and well-being, which can be life-changing.

The Long-Term Benefits of Emotional Work

By working with the subconscious mind, we start healing from the inside out. We're no longer just managing symptoms—we're changing the beliefs and emotional habits that led to them.

This is why emotional work has such long-term benefits: it helps us rebuild our inner foundation, making it easier to feel good consistently rather than experiencing ups and downs.

It makes us feel less anxious, and helps us feel happier and more positive. We can also trust more and start to expect good things in our lives and feel less impacted by the negative behaviors of others.

How the Subconscious Mind Works

It doesn't help to dive into emotional exercises without understanding *why* we are doing them and *how* they actually work.

First off, everything we think and feel comes from the subconscious. Anxiety, depression, awkwardness, love, hate, judgment etc. – it all comes from the subconscious.

Now, we know we need to change what the subconscious mind believes is true about us. But how do we do it? Most people hop onto positive affirmations, but they don't work on their own. They don't work because the subconscious mind doesn't speak regular English, so chanting positive affirmations is talking to your *conscious* mind which does speak regular English but doesn't make the decisions. Doing conscious mind exercises isn't effective. It's like asking a cashier at a store to give you a job when in fact, it's the manager you need to speak with. Your conscious mind is just the cashier doing the day-to-day stuff. The subconscious mind is the manager who makes the decisions.

To speak to the subconscious mind, we must tap into its language. It's proven that the subconscious speaks in **images + emotion.** I've put that in bold because it is an equation – you can't just use images alone. It won't work. And you can't use emotion alone. It won't work. But when you pair images and emotions, you can get the message to the subconscious.

Doing it once is like telling it a story. It may understand the message but it's not going to remember it.

Doing it 7 times will help it start to learn the story by heart.

But doing it 21 times or more is enough time to start developing new neural pathways to start forming new habits. While 21 days is a good starting point, if you can do these exercises for 42 days, you're more likely to succeed.

Now that you understand the exercises we'll focus on, we can move on to doing the actual exercises.

Practical Work

There are 2 subconscious reprogramming exercises that you must complete every single day for the next 21 days.

Follow these steps:

1. Make a list of your core wounds.

Here's a table showing the most common ones. Select the ones that most apply to you and add more if they aren't shown in this table.

I am not enough	I am abandoned	I am alone
I am unloved	I am bad	I am weak
I am unsafe	I am stupid/foolish	I am unworthy
I am helpless	I am unseen	I am unheard
I am unimportant	I am defective	I don't belong
I am disliked	I am misunderstood	I am disconnected
I am excluded	I am disrespected	I am rejected
I am trapped/stuck	I am powerless	I have no control

My Core Wounds Are:

_____

_____

_____

_____

_____

_____

_____

_____

_____

_____

_____

_____

_____

_____

_____

_____

_____

_____

_____

_____

_____

_____

_____

_____

_____

_____

_____

What if you don't know what your core wounds are?

A simple technique is to:

Think of the last 3 to 5 negative experiences you had. For example, you got into an argument with someone because they wanted you to go on an outing you weren't keen on going on. You weren't feeling good and eventually, you brought it up and wanted to leave. It turned into an argument.

Write down the details of the situation and argument.

Then, write down what story you have told yourself about that situation.

Perhaps the fact that you felt pushed into doing something you didn't want to do made you feel *I am unheard* or *I have no control*.

That's how you get down to what your core wounds are. It's best to do this exercise in private as that's when we can be really truthful about the stories negative situations in our lives lead us to believe about ourselves.

Your list should consist of a few negative core beliefs you have. Now we can get to work. Now we can get to work.

Negative Experiences and What They've Made Me Believe

_____

_____

_____

_____

_____

_____

_____

_____

_____

_____

_____

_____

_____

_____

_____

_____

_____

_____

_____

_____

_____

_____

_____

_____

_____

_____

_____

_____

_____

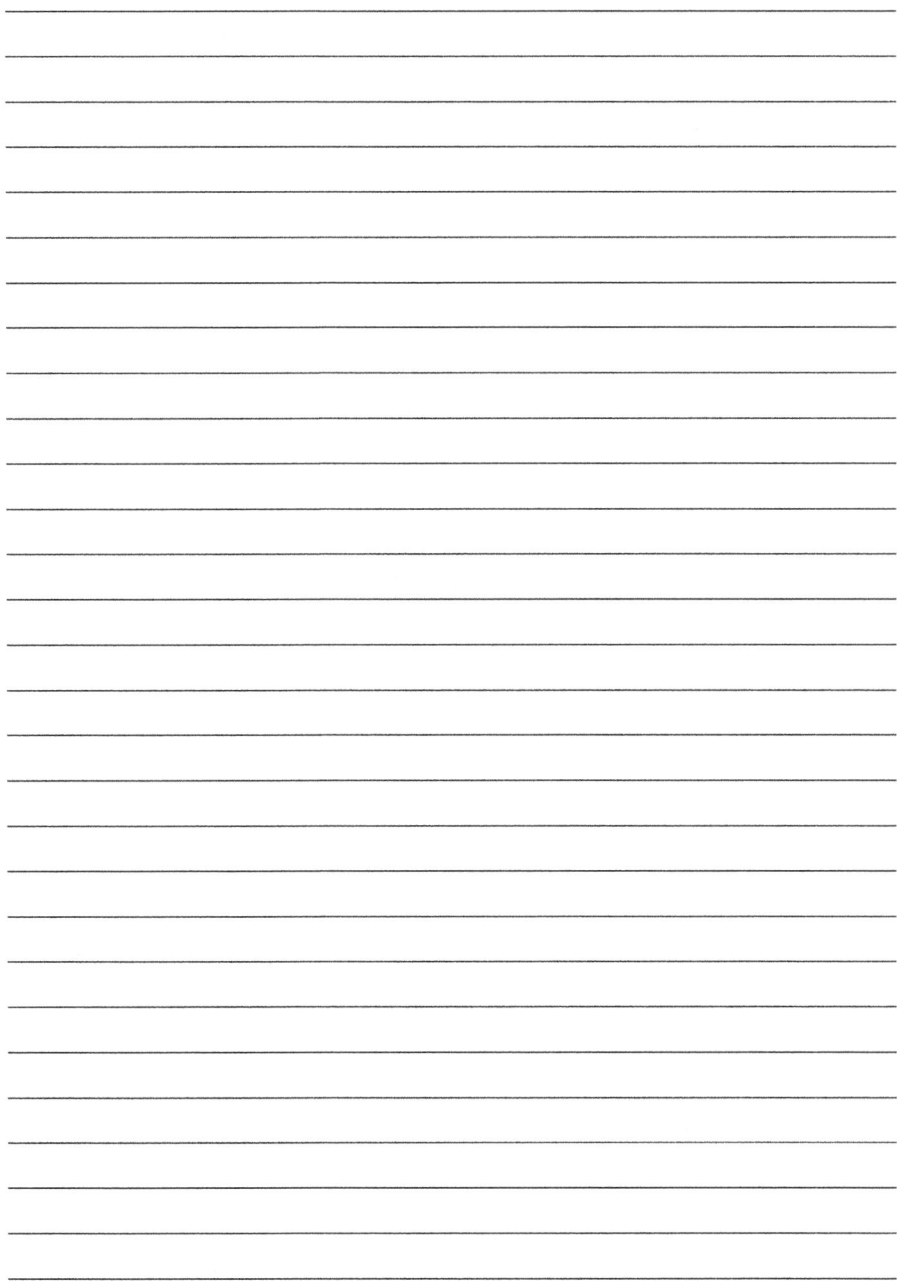

2. Next, write down the list of negative core wounds/beliefs.

Then directly next to it, reframe these beliefs with the opposing positive belief.

You should only use positive phrases here.

For example, a list might look like this:

I am not enough – I am enough and worthy
I am disliked – I am attractive and liked
I am abandoned – I am supported

Make sure that you use only positive phrasing. Using positive phrasing has a bigger impact on the subconscious.

For instance, you wouldn't say "I am not disliked" if your negative belief is "I am disliked."

You would say, "I am liked and appreciated" or something similar – it's best to use your own words here as your subconscious will understand your phrasing.

Just avoid all negative words altogether.

Positively Reframing My Negative Core Beliefs

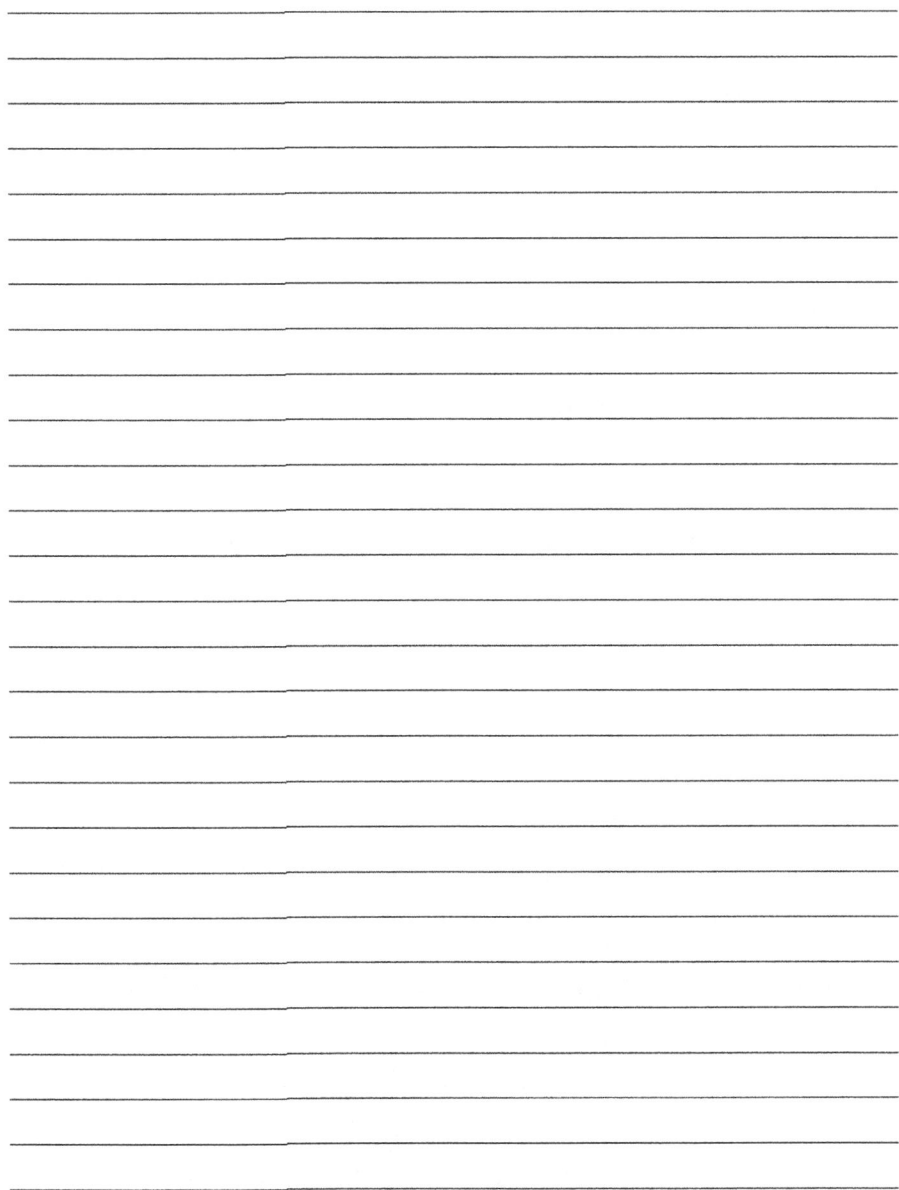

Prepping Your Core Wound Work Journal

At the end of this book, you will find a section titled **"Daily Core Wound Journal."**

On the first page (day 1) at the top where there's space for **"My new beliefs"**, copy all the opposing positive beliefs onto the first page. We are going to be working on programming your subconscious mind to believe these positive things and drive change forcibly. We need to be realistic. Don't go putting "I am a supermodel" or "I am a high-demand lawyer" there because the subconscious is a sniffer dog for BS and will reject it. That's all you do on this page for now. We will come back to these pages later.

Create a vision of the future recording.

Explanation.

Because the subconscious mind communicates in **images + emotions**, we are going to talk to it in that language and we are going in hard. We're going to use your voice, which the subconscious knows and finds safety in. And we're going to use your own core beliefs and needs against it. Sounds rough but when an addict wants the heroin (which is a good analogy for negative beliefs and thought loops) you must be hard on them to break the bad cycle. You're basically doing the same with your subconscious. You're taking the bad stuff away from it and while it will be uncomfortable to start, in a few weeks it will be thriving and healthy.

For the sake of our reprogramming efforts, we're going to focus on the wheel of life.

The **7 areas of life** framework is used in psychology and personal development to help people evaluate and improve their lives in a holistic, balanced way. The idea is that life is complex and focusing only on one or two areas (like career or health) without considering the others can lead to imbalances and dissatisfaction. By examining all seven areas, individuals can identify strengths, weaknesses, and areas for growth, making it a valuable tool for mental health professionals, coaches, and individuals working on personal growth.

In short, all humans need to have 7 healthy areas of life to be positive and thrive. If we neglect certain areas, we will find our lives unbalanced and lacking (are you noticing a theme here? We need certain things to get rid of that lack mindset).

The 7 areas of life (and you'll have noticed them on the pages you just printed) are:

- Career
- Financial
- Mental
- Physical
- Emotional
- Spiritual

- Relationships

Using the pages to follow or using your computer/laptop, get to work on writing a story about your ideal life. Be realistic but also don't downplay it. You should focus on all these areas, but I'd recommend ordering the sections in order of priority for you. For instance, if you find relationships are more important to you than your career, then start by describing your relationships.

Tell the story as if you're telling a friend who hasn't seen you in years about how wonderful your life is. Don't use words like "I can't believe this is my life" etc. as that's telling the subconscious that you're lying.

Another thing you must focus on is **weaving your opposing positive beliefs** into the piece of writing.

An example to start off would be like this (this is just an example, if the positive beliefs we're trying to land are: *I am disconnected, I am ugly, I am disliked, I don't belong*) – I have highlighted where I have included these:

*"I am in the best physical health I have been in, in years and **I am really looking good** – people are commenting on how healthy and fit I am looking these days. I've been running every second day and my sleep has improved so much that I feel rested and refreshed when I wake up every day. I have also started making sure that dinner time is fun, where my daughter and I put on the music and whip*

*up a meal we've researched online together – we do this
every Thursday. It's made me feel **connected and loved**.
Right now, I can smell the morning coffee fragrance
wafting through the crisp air as I make breakfast for my
daughter and pack my lunch for the day. I head off every
weekday morning to my job, which I absolutely love.
Everyone at work is friendly and likable. We get along
really well, and **I feel like I belong**. I feel appreciated for
all the knowledge and experience I bring to the table. The
mornings are busy, but we have a sense of real
camaraderie..."*

The idea is to describe your ideal life using as much
descriptive wording as possible.

You don't have to be a talented writer to do this.

Your subconscious is you, so tell the story as you would to
your friend/partner etc. Use as many of the senses as
possible.

Talk about smells, tastes, things you hear, things you see.
You must cover all 7 areas of life and be really, really – I
cannot stress enough – really descriptive.

We're talking at least 2000 words here but even longer
would be great.

My Vision of the Future (Ideal Life Imagery)

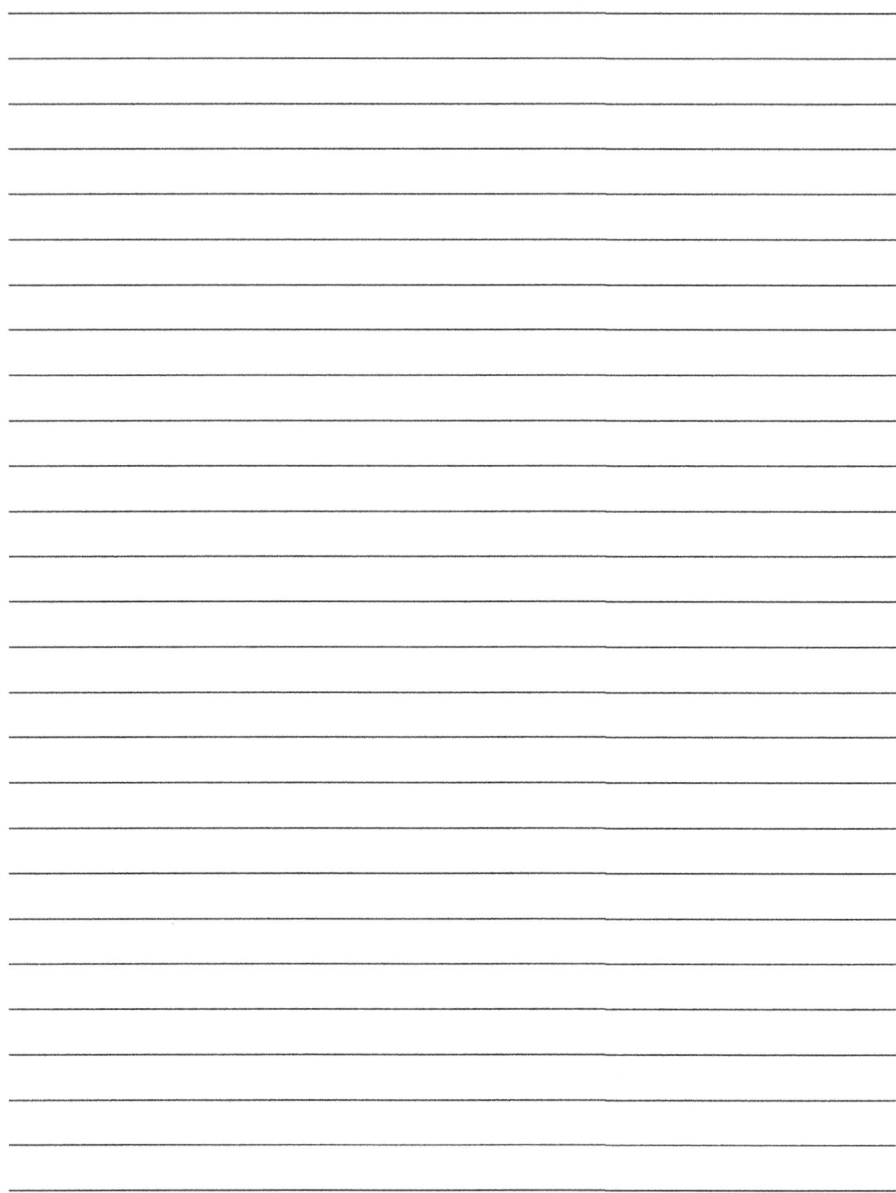

Now, grab your mobile phone and open the notes or recording feature, and slowly, read your piece of writing into a voice recording or note. Think of how slowly a hypnotist would talk.

We want this recording to be at least 10 minutes long. It doesn't have to be perfect – your subconscious isn't expecting that. My recording clearly sounds like I am reading it, but it still works. Try to keep a happy but relaxed tone and tempo, though – we want the subconscious to feel safe believing this story.

Your Daily Crib Sheet

Once you've completed your recording, it's time to make a crib sheet. On a post-it note, or a slip of paper – small enough to shove into the back of your phone cover or pocket, draw a line down the center.

On the one side, list the 7 areas of life. On the other side, list the opposing positive beliefs you will be working on (the ones that you've written on the top of your first page). You will carry this around with you all day, every day for the next 21 days.

We will come back to this in the instructions to follow.

Putting the Exercises Into Action

How to use your recording, 21 pages, and post-it note.

The concept is to use your entire day to start doing things that prove to the subconscious that the negative core beliefs it has are untrue and incorrect.

To start, your post-it note will play a role because you'll unlikely be overly familiar with the areas of life. You'll use it as a daytime crib sheet because you can only use your 21 printed pages **at the end of the day just before you go to sleep.**

Throughout the day, look for ways that you can drive your new positive beliefs into the 7 areas of life. You don't have to put *every* belief into every area.
But let's say you find a way to drive, "I am connected" into your relationships area of life. That's good enough.

You can focus on other beliefs to filter into other areas then. You may find that you filter multiple beliefs into one area and the same belief into several areas – that's fine.

You must ensure that each belief is used once, and that each area of life has something assigned to it. It's like a game you're playing with your brain. It will take a few days and suddenly your subconscious will start to like the game and will want to win it. It's a rewarding feeling when that kicks in.

I'll provide an example to illustrate the point. You really can be as creative as possible but I'm just providing some of my own so you can get some inspiration.

You don't write these down during the day because your main focus is to strategize and take action. The core beliefs for this example are:

I am enough
I am connected
I am attractive
I am capable
I am smart

You may have the following thoughts in your head while looking at your post-it crib note every now and then:

Financial: I think I need to find ways to cut back on unnecessary expenses today.

Career: I'd like to get a job I enjoy. I should probably study.

Physical: I should probably shave my legs and refresh my hair color. I could do with a run.

Personal development: I haven't paid attention to creating content in a while – maybe I need to study a new skill and teach it.

Relationships: it's really busy in the office today, I'll make everyone a cup of coffee/tea to ease their day a little.

With this list, and your strategizing and taking action throughout the day, you'll be having an inner dialogue with yourself, trying to find things you can do in each area of life that can prove that the negative core beliefs you have are untrue and start forcing the subconscious to believe that the positive beliefs are true.

The subconscious is a good investigator, so it wants to see proof. By thinking these strategies through and then actually *doing* things (taking action) to drive them home, you'll be giving the subconscious undeniable proof that what it's seeing is real and so the negative stories it's been telling you (and itself) simply cannot be true.

You'll notice over time anxiety easing because the subconscious eases up on the protect mode setting, too.

Your Evening Exercises – 21 Days

You'll need to make a routine of setting 20 to 30 minutes aside every evening when you climb into bed.

Keeping this workbook next to your bed is a good way to ensure you don't forget.

I always recommend doing these exercises just before bed because it's like a good debriefing for the day.

It's like giving the subconscious 21 days of end-of-day feedback packed with evidence to prove the new case you're demanding it buys into (the new positive beliefs).

The brain enters a different phase when you do your usual sleep routine and it's generally more susceptible to suggestion at this point, right before you go to sleep.

You will be using the pages at the back of this book for the next 21 days to complete this exercise.

Every day (night, should I say), you'll turn to the corresponding page and start by writing the core opposing positive beliefs you're focusing on the top.

They must be the same every single day.

Then, move to the next part of the page and start filling in the sections that focus on the 7 areas of life.

Here's an example of how someone might do this. You can be very creative with these.

You can say someone's interaction made you feel something, something that happened to you made you feel something, something you did made you feel something – there's no strict rule here.

The only focus is on providing proof that our new positive beliefs about ourselves are true.

Example to illustrate:

Are of Life	Core beliefs filtered in
Financial	• I felt capable today when I went through my bank statement and found old subscriptions I don't really use and canceled them. Now I'll have more financial stability going forward. • I proved I am capable of saving money when I purchased the lower-cost item instead of my favorite, most expensive one.
Career	• I am capable and smart because I smashed my interview presentation today. The interviewer told me that they'd never had someone so prepared and knowledgeable on the subject.

Physical	<ul><li>I feel attractive and likable because I did some self-care today. I moisturized, colored my hair, and whitened my teeth.</li><li>I went for a long walk to kickstart my exercise plans which made me feel like I am well on my way to becoming the attractive version of myself.</li></ul>
Mental	<ul><li>I am enough because today, I got out of bed on the first alarm and put on some positive high-energy music.</li><li>I am smart and interesting because I completed Wordle in 3 tries.</li></ul>
Emotional	<ul><li>I connected with xyz at work for a few minutes and made them smile. I feel liked and connected.</li><li>I feel capable of mastering my emotions because I stuck to the 21-day course and haven't missed a day for 14 days.</li></ul>
Relationships	<ul><li>I feel liked and loved because my friend xyz reached out and checked in on me. It's nice when people reach out because they care.</li></ul>
Spiritual/Personal Development	<ul><li>I feel enough, connected, and capable because I started looking into how the law of attraction and vibration can help me develop into the positive person I am becoming.</li></ul>

They can be as simple as *"I feel liked because xyz at work made me a cup of tea or shared a joke with me."*

The idea is to start super basic. Sometimes being enough is doing something small or feeling appreciated for something small. If someone makes you feel appreciated, remember that. It's proof that you're enough!

Second Exercise for the Evening

Once you have completed writing these sections when in bed, it's time to put your vision of future recording to work.

You'll need earphones.

Get comfy in bed, pop your earphones in, and listen to your story. It's quite important to imagine the pictures/video/imagery in your mind while you listen to your story. You may find that you start falling asleep while listening to your recording after a few days of practice - that's fine.

You must do this at night before sleep.

It's also a good idea to listen to it on the way to work/school too. Nighttime listening is the most important though. Listening on the way to work is a boost and will really help but it's not the main focus of our exercise.

** You must do both exercises every single day for the next 21 days.

If you skip a day, you will need to start from day 1 again, so focus on making it part of your daily routine. Setting an alarm on your mobile for bedtime to remind you may be needed when you first get started.

You will find the 21-day journal on the next page.

Now that you're prepared to start the exercises, you can get started.

Reach out and let me know how you've done after the 21-day reprogramming period.

If you liked this workbook and the information included, leave a positive review on Amazon for me – it keeps me inspired!

Best of luck!

Molly
Ps. Connect with me on Medium:
https://medium.com/@my-avoidant-ex

Day 1: _____**(date)**

My new beliefs:

_____
_____
_____
_____

Spiritual/Personal Development:

_____
_____
_____
_____

Emotional:

_____
_____
_____
_____

Career:

_____
_____
_____
_____

Finances:

_____

_____

_____

_____

_____

Relationships:

_____

_____

_____

_____

_____

Mental:

_____

_____

_____

_____

_____

Physical:

_____

_____

_____

_____

_____

Day 2: _____(date)

My new beliefs:

_____
_____
_____
_____

Spiritual/Personal Development:

_____
_____
_____
_____

Emotional:

_____
_____
_____
_____

Career:

_____
_____
_____
_____

Finances:

_____

_____

_____

_____

_____

Relationships:

_____

_____

_____

_____

_____

Mental:

_____

_____

_____

_____

_____

Physical:

_____

_____

_____

_____

_____

Day 3: _____**(date)**

My new beliefs:

_____
_____
_____
_____

Spiritual/Personal Development:

_____
_____
_____
_____

Emotional:

_____
_____
_____
_____

Career:

_____
_____
_____
_____

Finances:

_____

_____

_____

_____

_____

Relationships:

_____

_____

_____

_____

_____

Mental:

_____

_____

_____

_____

_____

Physical:

_____

_____

_____

_____

_____

Day 4: _____**(date)**

My new beliefs:

_____
_____
_____
_____

Spiritual/Personal Development:

_____
_____
_____
_____

Emotional:

_____
_____
_____
_____

Career:

_____
_____
_____
_____

Finances:

_____

_____

_____

_____

_____

Relationships:

_____

_____

_____

_____

_____

Mental:

_____

_____

_____

_____

_____

Physical:

_____

_____

_____

_____

_____

Day 5: _____(date)

My new beliefs:

_____
_____
_____
_____

Spiritual/Personal Development:

_____
_____
_____
_____

Emotional:

_____
_____
_____
_____

Career:

_____
_____
_____
_____

Finances:

_____

_____

_____

_____

_____

Relationships:

_____

_____

_____

_____

_____

Mental:

_____

_____

_____

_____

_____

Physical:

_____

_____

_____

_____

_____

Day 6: _____**(date)**

My new beliefs:

_____
_____
_____
_____

Spiritual/Personal Development:

_____
_____
_____
_____

Emotional:

_____
_____
_____
_____

Career:

_____
_____
_____
_____

Finances:

_____
_____
_____
_____
_____

Relationships:

_____
_____
_____
_____
_____

Mental:

_____
_____
_____
_____
_____

Physical:

_____
_____
_____
_____
_____

Day 7: _____(date)

My new beliefs:

_____
_____
_____
_____

Spiritual/Personal Development:

_____
_____
_____
_____

Emotional:

_____
_____
_____
_____

Career:

_____
_____
_____
_____

Finances:

_____
_____
_____
_____
_____

Relationships:

_____
_____
_____
_____
_____

Mental:

_____
_____
_____
_____
_____

Physical:

_____
_____
_____
_____
_____

Day 8: _____(date)

My new beliefs:

_____
_____
_____
_____

Spiritual/Personal Development:

_____
_____
_____
_____

Emotional:

_____
_____
_____
_____

Career:

_____
_____
_____
_____

Finances:

_____

_____

_____

_____

_____

Relationships:

_____

_____

_____

_____

_____

Mental:

_____

_____

_____

_____

_____

Physical:

_____

_____

_____

_____

_____

Day 9: _____**(date)**

My new beliefs:

_____

_____

_____

_____

Spiritual/Personal Development:

_____

_____

_____

_____

Emotional:

_____

_____

_____

_____

Career:

_____

_____

_____

_____

Finances:

_____

_____

_____

_____

_____

Relationships:

_____

_____

_____

_____

_____

Mental:

_____

_____

_____

_____

_____

Physical:

_____

_____

_____

_____

_____

Day 10:

_____(date)

My new beliefs:

_____
_____
_____
_____

Spiritual/Personal Development:

_____
_____
_____
_____

Emotional:

_____
_____
_____
_____

Career:

_____
_____
_____
_____

Finances:

_____
_____
_____
_____
_____

Relationships:

_____
_____
_____
_____
_____

Mental:

_____
_____
_____
_____
_____

Physical:

_____
_____
_____
_____
_____

Day 11: _____(date)

My new beliefs:

_____
_____
_____
_____

Spiritual/Personal Development:

_____
_____
_____
_____

Emotional:

_____
_____
_____
_____

Career:

_____
_____
_____
_____

Finances:

_____
_____
_____
_____
_____

Relationships:

_____
_____
_____
_____
_____

Mental:

_____
_____
_____
_____
_____

Physical:

_____
_____
_____
_____
_____

Day 12:_____**(date)**

My new beliefs:

_____

_____

_____

_____

Spiritual/Personal Development:

_____

_____

_____

_____

Emotional:

_____

_____

_____

_____

Career:

_____

_____

_____

_____

Finances:

_____

_____

_____

_____

_____

Relationships:

_____

_____

_____

_____

_____

Mental:

_____

_____

_____

_____

_____

Physical:

_____

_____

_____

_____

_____

Day 13: _____(date)

My new beliefs:

_____
_____
_____
_____

Spiritual/Personal Development:

_____
_____
_____
_____
_____

Emotional:

_____
_____
_____
_____

Career:

_____
_____
_____
_____
_____

Finances:

_____

_____

_____

_____

_____

Relationships:

_____

_____

_____

_____

_____

Mental:

_____

_____

_____

_____

_____

Physical:

_____

_____

_____

_____

_____

Day 14: _____**(date)**

My new beliefs:

_____
_____
_____
_____

Spiritual/Personal Development:

_____
_____
_____
_____

Emotional:

_____
_____
_____
_____

Career:

_____
_____
_____
_____

Finances:

_____
_____
_____
_____
_____

Relationships:

_____
_____
_____
_____
_____

Mental:

_____
_____
_____
_____
_____

Physical:

_____
_____
_____
_____
_____

Day 15: _____(date)

My new beliefs:

_____
_____
_____
_____

Spiritual/Personal Development:

_____
_____
_____
_____
_____

Emotional:

_____
_____
_____
_____
_____

Career:

_____
_____
_____
_____
_____

Finances:

_____
_____
_____
_____
_____

Relationships:

_____
_____
_____
_____
_____

Mental:

_____
_____
_____
_____
_____

Physical:

_____
_____
_____
_____
_____

Day 16: _____(date)

My new beliefs:

_____
_____
_____
_____

Spiritual/Personal Development:

_____
_____
_____
_____
_____

Emotional:

_____
_____
_____
_____
_____

Career:

_____
_____
_____
_____
_____

Finances:

_____

_____

_____

_____

_____

Relationships:

_____

_____

_____

_____

_____

Mental:

_____

_____

_____

_____

_____

Physical:

_____

_____

_____

_____

_____

Day 17: _____(date)

My new beliefs:

_____
_____
_____
_____

Spiritual/Personal Development:

_____
_____
_____
_____

Emotional:

_____
_____
_____
_____

Career:

_____
_____
_____
_____

Finances:

_____

_____

_____

_____

_____

Relationships:

_____

_____

_____

_____

_____

Mental:

_____

_____

_____

_____

_____

Physical:

_____

_____

_____

_____

_____

_____

Day 18: _____(date)

My new beliefs:

_____
_____
_____
_____

Spiritual/Personal Development:

_____
_____
_____
_____

Emotional:

_____
_____
_____
_____

Career:

_____
_____
_____
_____

Finances:

_____

_____

_____

_____

_____

Relationships:

_____

_____

_____

_____

_____

Mental:

_____

_____

_____

_____

_____

Physical:

_____

_____

_____

_____

_____

Day 19: _____(date)

My new beliefs:

_____
_____
_____
_____

Spiritual/Personal Development:

_____
_____
_____
_____

Emotional:

_____
_____
_____
_____

Career:

_____
_____
_____
_____

Finances:

_____

_____

_____

_____

_____

Relationships:

_____

_____

_____

_____

_____

Mental:

_____

_____

_____

_____

_____

Physical:

_____

_____

_____

_____

_____

Day 20: _____(date)

My new beliefs:

_____
_____
_____
_____

Spiritual/Personal Development:

_____
_____
_____
_____

Emotional:

_____
_____
_____
_____

Career:

_____
_____
_____
_____

Finances:

_____
_____
_____
_____
_____

Relationships:

_____
_____
_____
_____
_____

Mental:

_____
_____
_____
_____
_____

Physical:

_____
_____
_____
_____
_____

Day 21: _____(date)

My new beliefs:

_____
_____
_____
_____

Spiritual/Personal Development:

_____
_____
_____
_____

Emotional:

_____
_____
_____
_____

Career:

_____
_____
_____
_____

Finances:

_____
_____
_____
_____
_____

Relationships:

_____
_____
_____
_____
_____

Mental:

_____
_____
_____
_____
_____

Physical:

_____
_____
_____
_____
_____

Made in the USA
Coppell, TX
28 April 2025

48768121R00056